W9-BNE-696

MEL BAY'S FINGERPICKING GOSPEL SOLOS

by
Craig Dobbins

CD Contents

1 Glory To His Name [1:41]

2 Come, Thou Fount of Every Blessing [2:05]

3 Wayfaring Stranger [1:41]

4 Love Lifted Me [2:23]

5 When We All Get To Heaven [1:27]

6 Must Jesus Bear the Cross Alone? [1:11]

1 2 3 4 5 6 7 8 9 0

Visit us on the Web at http://www.melbay.com — E-mail us at email@melbay.com

MEL BAY

Book Contents

Acknowledgments

Special thanks to Clyde Kendrick, whose advice, assistance, and generosity have been invaluable to me.

Thanks also to my wife, Julie, for her encouragement and help, and to my good friend Dr. Larry Kilgore.

Photography by David Moon.

Guitars by: Gibson, Kirk Sand, and Taylor.

Introduction

These are some of my favorite hymns and gospel songs, set to a fingerpickin' style. I hope you enjoy learning and playing them, whether for family and friends, for your church, or just for fun.

I would like to acknowledge Chet Atkins, Jerry Reed, and Paul Yandell, whose playing continues to inspire me and so many other guitarists.

If you have any questions or comments, please contact me c/o Acoustic Guitar Workshop, P.O. Box 8075, Gadsden, AL 35902.

Glory To His Name

Down at the cross where my savior died
Down where for cleansing from sin I cried
There to my heart was the blood applied
Glory to His name!

"But God forbid that I should glory, save in the cross of our Lord Jesus Christ." -Galatians 6:14

About the music . . .

This gospel song was written by two preachers, E.A. Hoffman and J.H. Stockton. Hoffman wrote or co-wrote many hymns and gospel songs, including *Are You Washed in the Blood?* and *Leaning On the Everlasting Arms.*

Performance notes . . .

I begin by playing a verse freely, in a pseudo-classic style. Just before the chorus (at measure 7), I switch to thumbstyle, muting the bass strings with the heel of my right hand. The music changes from 4/4 to cut time here, so be sure to pick up the tempo.

At measure 28, I play a verse Carter style, leading with my thumb and brushing with my fingers. I "borrowed" the lick in measures 36 and 37 from **Chet Atkins'** version of *Wildwood Flower.*

After another chorus, I take the coda. I slow down at measure 49, and linger on the F7 chord in measure 51. The lick in measures 51 and 52 was inspired by **Jerry Reed**.

About the recording . . .

I used a Taylor 514-C steel string acoustic, equipped with a Fishman Matrix pickup.

"Glory to His Name" Chords

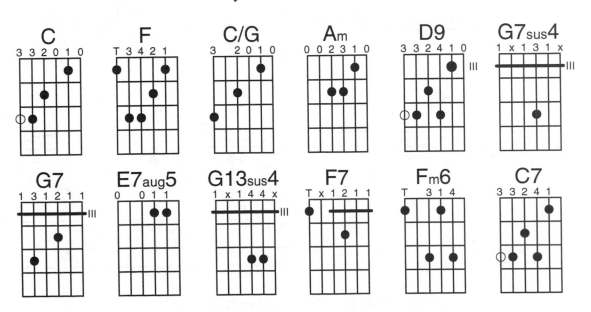

Glory To His Name

Words by E.A. Hoffman

Music by J.H. Stockton
Arranged by Craig B. Dobbins

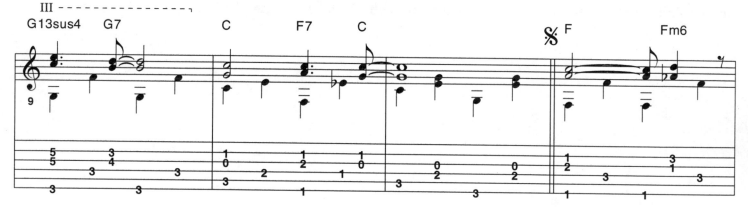

Glory To His Name

Glory To His Name

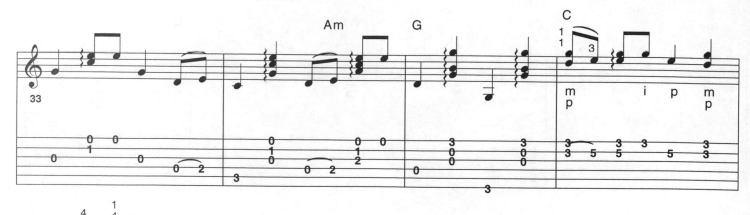

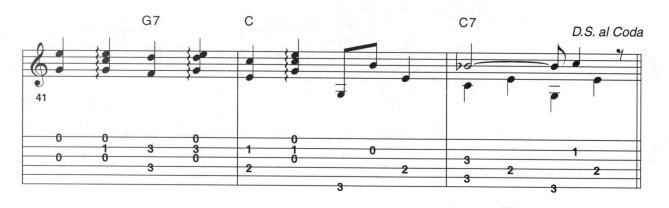

6

Glory To His Name

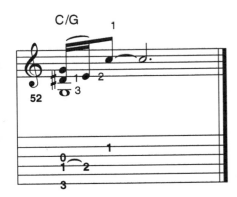

*This page has been
left blank to avoid
awkward page turns*

Come, Thou Fount of Every Blessing

Come thou Fount of every blessing, tune my heart to sing Thy grace
Streams of mercy, never ceasing, call for songs of loudest praise

"For with Thee is the fountain of life." -Psalm 36:9

About the music . . .

The text was written by Robert Robinson in 1758. John Wyeth included it in his *Repository of Sacred Music, Part Second* in 1813.

Performance notes . . .

My arrangement of this majestic hymn has just a touch of Celtic flavor. The dropped D tuning (D A D G B E, 6th-1st strings) not only extends the range of the guitar, but it also gives me two D strings to use as "drones," or sustaining notes.

The first time through, I play the melody line alone, accompanied by an occasional bass note or two. Watch out for the "ornaments"- the hammers, pull-offs, and slides.

At the pickup to measure 17, I go up an octave, introducing a simple harmony line below the melody. Only in measures 28-30 do I use full chords. Then, it's back to simple harmonies, and finally, to the melody, once again in the lower octave.

About the recording . . .

I used a Kirk Sand nylon string electric.

Come, Thou Fount of Every Blessing

Words by Robert Robinson

Music by John Wyeth
Arranged by Craig B. Dobbins

6th string to D

Come, Thou Fount of Every Blessing

Wayfaring Stranger

I am a poor wayfaring stranger
While traveling through this world of woe
But there's no sickness, toil, or danger
In that bright world to which I go.

" . . . they were strangers and pilgrims on the earth." -Hebrews 11:13

About the music . . .

One of my favorite traditional gospel tunes.

Performance notes . . .

When necessary, I use thumb and fingers together to play the downstem notes, as in measure 1.

I use my thumb to fret the Dm/F chord in measures 5 and 6, and elsewhere.

On the E7 chord in measure 8, I rake the 1st-5th strings with my index finger, followed by a downstroke on the 6th string with my thumb.

Don't be afraid of the 5th fret F chord in measures 17 and 18. It's like a C position, capoed at the 5th fret- only your 1st finger is the capo.

Watch both left and right hand fingering on the descending scale in measures 29-30. That's an artificial harmonic in measure 30. Touch the string 12 frets above the tab number with the tip of your right index finger and play the note with your thumb.

On the recording, I play the bridge section twice.

About the recording . . .

I used a Kirk sand nylon-string electric.

"Wayfaring Stranger" Chords

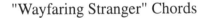
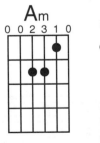

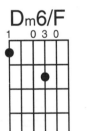
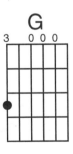
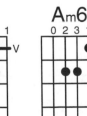

Wayfaring Stranger

Traditional
Arranged by Craig B. Dobbins

14

Wayfaring Stranger

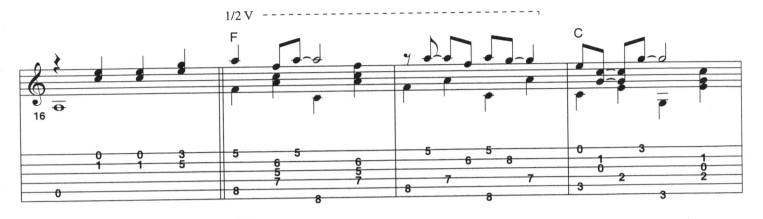

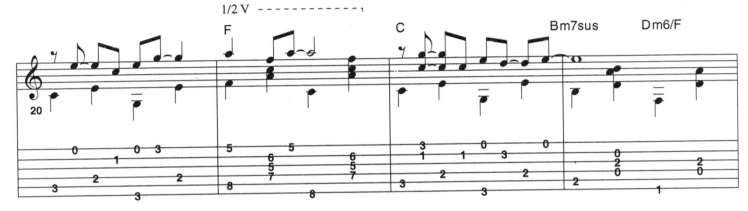

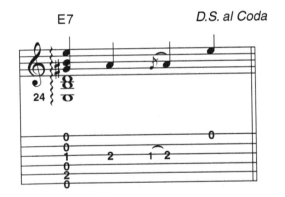

Wayfaring Stranger

Love Lifted Me

When nothing else could help, Love lifted me.
"And Jesus took him by the hand, and lifted him up." -Mark 9:27

About the music . . .

Written in 1912 by James Rowe and Howard E. Smith.

Performance notes . . .

I tried for a "gospel piano" feel here. Watch the grace notes, and above all, don't rush!

Throughout the song, I anticipate notes on the 3rd and 4th strings by playing the note slightly ahead of the beat. For example, in measure 1, I play the E note (3rd string, 9th fret) just before the rest of the chord. In measure 2, I anticipate the G# note (4th string, 6th fret).

The music takes you through the chorus twice, with a little variation the second time around. There *is* a verse (*"I was sinking deep in sin, far from the peaceful shore . . ."*), but I didn't transcribe it here. Maybe *you* can finish it.

By the way, that's a **Jerry Reed** lick in measures 73-75.

About the recording . . .

I used a Gibson Country Gentleman electric. I recorded this one with my bare thumb (no thumbpick), to get a smoother sound on the bass strings.

Love Lifted Me

Words by James Rowe

Music by Howard E. Smith
Arranged by Craig B. Dobbins

Love Lifted Me

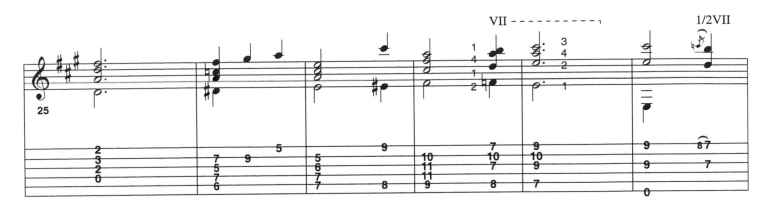

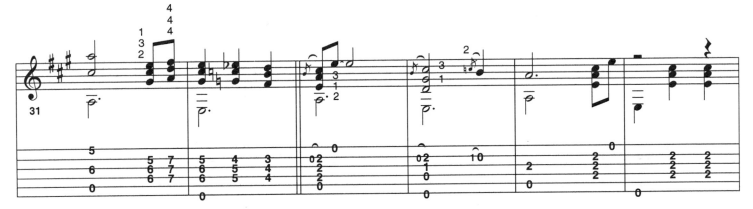

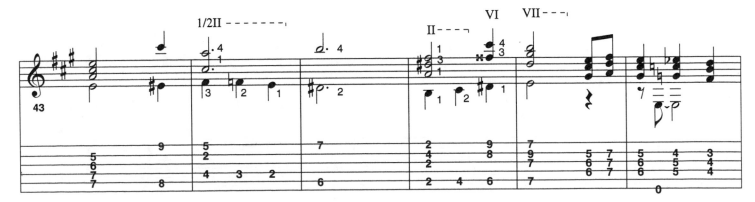

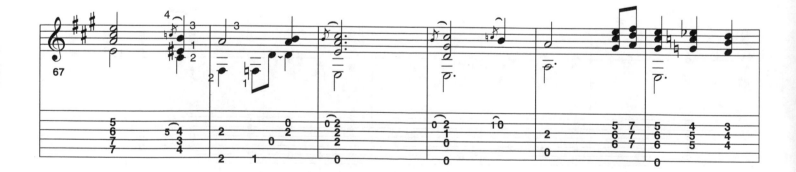

Love Lifted Me

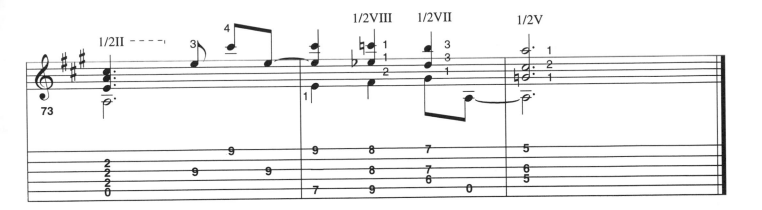

This page has been
left blank to avoid
awkward page turns

When We All Get To Heaven

When we all get to heaven, what a day of rejoicing that will be
When we all see Jesus, we'll sing and shout the victory.

"Eye hath not seen, nor ear heard, neither have entered into the heart of man, the things which God hath prepared for them that love him." -I Corinthians 2:9

About the music . . .

Written in 1898 by Eliza E. Hewitt and Emily D. Wilson.

Performance notes . . .

For my arrangement of this classic gospel tune I chose the key of A, always a good choice for thumbstyle pickin'.

For the intro, I play a verse freely. Notice the moving bass line. At the chorus (measure 9), I switch to thumbstyle. Remember the change from 4/4 to cut time.

I use my thumb to fret the D note (6th string, 10th fret) in measures 21-22 and elsewhere.

I "tag" the chorus at measure 58, and slip in a little fancy fingerwork at measure 64. It's a roll pattern (i-p-i-m) that **Chet Atkins** has used many times.

About the recording . . .

I used a Gibson Chet Atkins Country Gentleman electric.

"When We All Get to Heaven" Chords

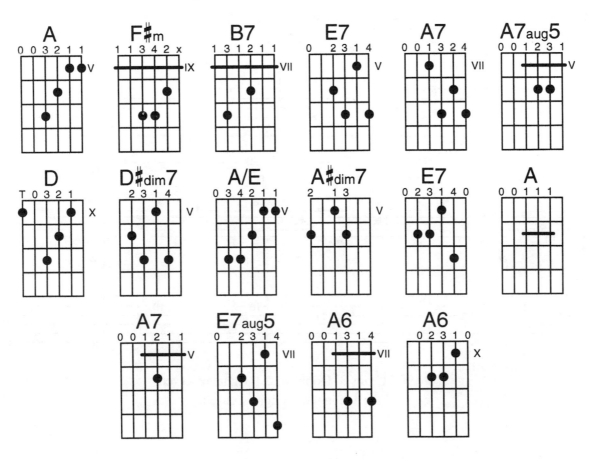

When We All Get to Heaven

Words by Eliza E. Hewitt

Music by Emily D. Wilson
Arranged by Craig B. Dobbins

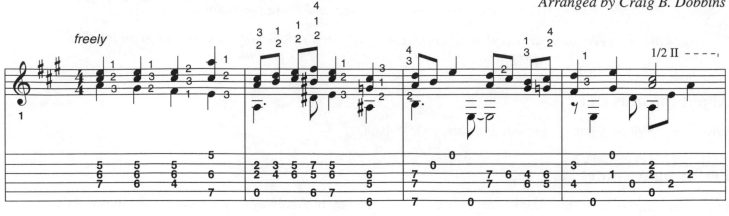

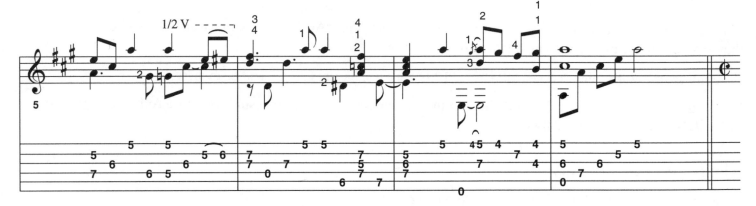

When We All Get To Heaven

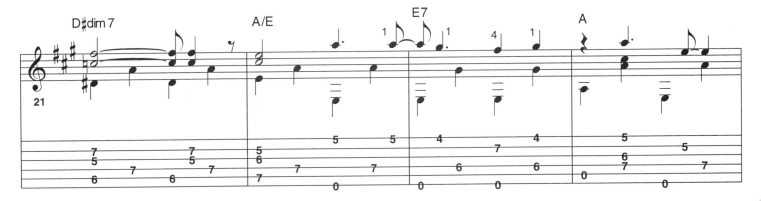

When We All Get To Heaven

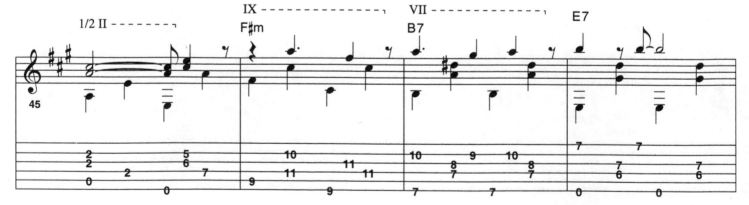

When We All Get To Heaven

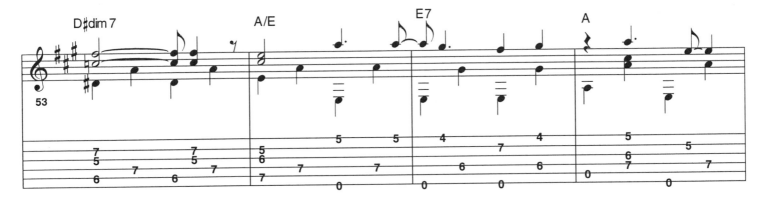

When We All Get To Heaven

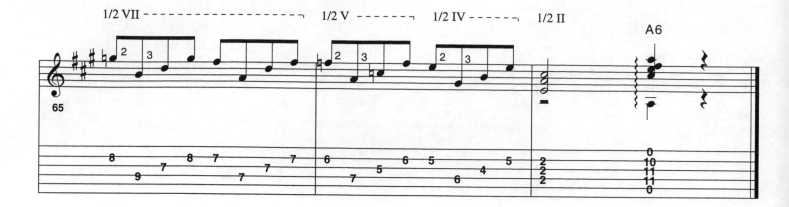

Must Jesus Bear the Cross Alone?

Must Jesus bear the cross alone, and all the world go free?
No, there's a cross for everyone, and there's a cross for me.

"Then Jesus said unto his disciples, If any man will come after me, let him deny himself, and take up his cross, and follow me." -Matthew 16:25

About the music . . .

George N. Allen composed this beautiful melody in 1844. The text was written by Thomas Shepherd in 1855. The melody reminds me of another gospel song, *Precious Lord, Take My Hand*.

Performance notes . . .

In this arrangement, I tried to keep the bass line moving, and used passing tones between chords. My favorite move is the F♯7 to B7 turnaround in measures 6 and 7. At the pickup to measure 17, I dropped the accompaniment for a measure, for emphasis.

Those are harmonics in measure 25. Touch the string 12 frets above the tab number with the tip of your right index finger and play the note with your thumb.

Play freely, and try to make the melody "sing" above the accompaniment.

About the recording . . .

I used a Kirk Sand nylon-string electric.

"Must Jesus Bear the Cross Alone" Chords

Must Jesus Bear the Cross Alone?

Words by Thomas Shepherd

Music by George N. Allen

Arranged by Craig B. Dobbins

Must Jesus Bear the Cross Alone?

About the Author

Craig Dobbins lives in Gadsden, Alabama, with his wife Julie, and son Craig Bennett Jr. His books and recordings include *The Guitar Style of Jerry Reed*, *Fingerpickin' Guitar Solos*, *Hymns for Fingerstyle Guitar*, and *Down Home Picking*. He has written for such publications as *Acoustic Guitar* magazine, *Fingerstyle Guitar* magazine and *Mister Guitar* (journal of the Chet Atkins Appreciation Society).

Craig also writes and publishes *Acoustic Guitar Workshop*, a quarterly instructional package featuring fingerstyle arrangements in notation and tab, with teaching comments and cassette.

For information, please write Craig c/o Acoustic Guitar Workshop, P.O. Box 8075, Gadsden AL, 35902.